Vidhi Bubna is an award-winning journalist. She is also a vocal women's rights activist and has been awarded at the Parliament of the United Kingdom twice for her work. She was invited by HM King Charles to attend the Commonwealth Day Ceremony at Westminster Abbey in London. As a journalist, Vidhi has researched extensively on women's rights movements and their influence on the world. She has been inducted into several leading societies across the world including the Royal Society of Arts, Queen's Commonwealth Trust and George Bush's Points of Lights Foundation as a 2021 honoree. When Vidhi is not writing, you are likely to find her at a museum or an art gallery. She resides in Central London and hopes to move to the United States soon.

Praise for the Book

"Creative and courageous" – Namita Gokhale, writer, co-founder, Jaipur Literature Festival

"An eye-opening book – bold and courageous. It captures something everyone can resonate with across the globe and has experienced at a deeper level: identity struggle."
– Sandeep Das, bestselling author, social media influencer, leading columnist, *The Times of India, Economic Times* and *Forbes*

"What an engaging read! Women often bottle up these feelings that you have so beautifully written out. When you need some quiet time with yourself, to reflect upon life ...this just brings out your emotions in words that you can easily picturise because all women, no matter what age, caste, creed, social status have undergone at least some in their lifetime!"
– Jayashree Narayanan, journalist, *Indian Express*

"A new way of delving deep into gender equality by being the past, present and the future"
– Ambassador Anil Trigunayat (IFS Retired), former Indian Ambassador to Jordan, Libya and Malta

"Ground-breaking work in gender equality. Much needed to make the world a better place"
– Yash Sardesai, CEO, Sri Lanka Legends

"Poignant, moving and beautifully worded, this anthology of poetry ought to be read by men and women of all ages."
– Mohamed Zeeshan, author of *Flying Blind: India's Quest for Global Leadership,* foreign affairs columnist at *The Diplomat*

"Very fine at times, disturbing, almost poignant poetry. The expressions of emotion of love or longing go with a deeper disquiet with a world where women's own emotive space and dignity struggle to achieve a voice. That voice is distinctive in this debut anthology"
— Mahesh Rangarajan, Rhodes Scholar, ex-dean of academic affairs, Ashoka University

"Incisive, thought provoking and powerful. Each page gives you something to ponder all day"
— Krishanu Ranwan, founder, Public Policy Network

"Rich, elegantly written, moving text about the struggles women face on a daily basis. This book will spark conversations to bring change"
— Anoop Keshari, founder of the Instagram page Impractical_1

"A deeply visceral book that holds a mirror to the anxieties of our age, *The Culture Trap* is perceptive, powerful and poignant. The poems not only reinstate the adage that the personal is the political but also shed light on what it means to discover oneself in the midst of a zeitgeist that is confusing and compelling in equal measure. A must-read for anyone who wishes to understand their own emotions better."
— Priyam Marik, journalist and media consultant based in Kolkata, columnist for *The Telegraph*

"Empowering and healing at the same time, *The Culture Trap* feels like facing my own journey."
— Vrinda Rastogi, features writer, *GlobalSpa Magazine*

"*The Culture Trap* is a must-read. It will potentially create ground for greater gender equality. The author has written it with sensitivity, compassion and a deep understanding about the struggles faced by women across the world. A very pertinent and thought-provoking book."
— Rrashima Swaarup Verma, senior corporate analyst, popular columnist and bestselling author

"Gender truths revealed in lyrical rhymes that are unabashedly raw and revealing."
    – Erica D'Souza, prime time radio host and media personality

"The book is beautifully written, creatively emphasising the struggles and battles which are especially trapping for women. Impactful, full of wit and engaging. A must-read."
    – Husnal Bhasin, student at Columbia University, mental health advocate

"*The Culture Trap* is a must-read for everyone who is pushing to make the world a more gender-equal place or for anyone who has ever experienced sexism or has been baffled by it in their life."
    – Srinath Rao P., founding editor, *The ArmChair Journal*

"An overview of how profound differences experienced between boys and girls shape the way they respond to society. It helps develop an insightful perception about the sexist culture that impact women empowerment."
    – Kajol Sitani, strategy and communication, *Samhita Social Ventures*

"This book carries a fabulous, relevant and very important theme. Easy to read and relate to different stories via poems of people at different stages looking at their sexuality and relationships. The illustrations make it soothing and playful to the eye and lead to a lovely, healing book to have in your collection: to reread, resonate with in your way and even share with a teenager in your family to start important conversations!"
    – Jigyasa Taneja Sethi, award-winning film-maker

"Insightful, resonating and powerful poetry."
    – Sana Mittar, intern at the office of UN Secretary General, Diana award winner and founder and president of Global Volunteers Action Network

"A book that will speak to you and make you reflect deeply."
    – Dr Suruchi Mittar, business transformationist, HR strategist, people analytics, and leadership coach

THE CULTURE TRAP

Vidhi Bubna

Illustrations by Jenissa Paharia

Om Books International

First published in 2024 by

Om Books International

Corporate & Editorial Office
A-12, Sector 64, Noida 201 301
Uttar Pradesh, India
Phone: +91 120 477 4100
Email: editorial@ombooks.com
Website: www.ombooksinternational.com

Sales Office
107, Ansari Road, Darya Ganj
New Delhi 110 002, India
Phone: +91 11 4000 9000
Email: sales@ombooks.com
Website: www.ombooks.com

ISBN: 978-81-19750-28-3

Printed in India

10 9 8 7 6 5 4 3 2 1

This book is dedicated to my mother. And to several generations of women who have struggled in the face of gender inequality and done their bit to break free which has given me the power to be where I am today.

ACKNOWLEDGEMENTS

I would like to thank the 200 women from diverse parts of Rajasthan who agreed to talk to me about their real-life experiences. They opened up to me about their struggles, sometimes even violence and abuse, their hopes and their wildest dreams, the way they would perhaps want their life to be. Their words are what have fuelled this book and have created a stronger-than-ever urge in me to try to make a difference in society. I hope I have succeeded in making all the women I interviewed and spoke to heard in this book. I also hope I have successfully helped women across the world to feel that they are not alone in their journey. We have experienced something that is similar and must unite towards empowering ourselves and our sisters. Be it a small community, country or the world, all women have struggled in some way.

This book is also about me, it is about you, your sister, mother, grandmother, father, friend, family and the stranger you meet. Thank you, my dear reader, for making this book a part of your life. I have Jenissa Paharia to thank for the beautiful illustrations in this book which have made each page come alive. Each page has turned into a breathing organism with a distinct soul of its own. I am grateful to Shantanu Ray Chaudhuri from Om Books International for his support and my book agent The Book Bakers, Suhail Mathur, who believed in my work and ensured it reaches the right audience. I am also grateful to friends like Krishanu Ranwan, Anoop Keshari and Sanskruti Jain who looked at drafts of my work and offered me feedback. Professor Mahesh Rangarajan, for his overall impact on my life and the "Never Give Up" attitude he instilled in me. God only knows Professor Mahesh has picked me up at the lowest points in my life. Some other professors who have influenced my life positively include Dr Carolina Matos, Dr Anubha Sarkar and Dr Liza Schuster. Thank you for teaching me. I thank City University of London for making me believe in second chances and Ashoka University for being the first-ever real shot I got at feminism in my life. Being born was of course the first shot I got – thank you to my mother for bearing me for nine months in your belly. I know I give you very little credit for that.

Namita Gokhale has my gratitude for believing in my work and being one of the first people to endorse my book, which has led to the book having greater belief among the writers' community in general. She truly has the Midas touch. My immense gratitude to my family for giving me the space and time a human deserves, or as Virginia Woolf states "To have a room of one's own" to grow and shine, to experiment and explore, to understand and influence and finally to create an impact. Finally, special thanks to my best friend, Hans, who has always supported me in my journey and has lent a patient ear to everything I have to say. I love you.

INTRODUCTION

Rajasthan in India is a state of immense cultural heritage. Despite the rich history and culture, which of course cannot be ignored, Rajasthan also has a history of gender inequality and oppression. It happens to be the state with the largest gap between male and female literacy. According to a 2021 report in India Times, the gender divide in Rajasthan's literacy is almost 23.2 per cent. According to some unofficial reports which have even been quoted in Business Standard and other reputed publications, there are around 2,500 cases of female infanticide and foeticide every day in the state. These numbers are alarming and only go to showcase the harsh reality faced by women in Rajasthan. However, this is not just the story of women in Rajasthan, it is also the story of women across India and across the world at large.

I was born in Mumbai, a buzzing metropolis and the financial capital of India. However, I am a Marwari with ancestral roots in Rajasthan. This has given me a lifetime of dual experiences. I have been stuck in between two cultures: the culture of Mumbai, the city of dreams that begs freedom and individuality, and the Marwari culture of Rajasthan which promises lifelong tradition and promotes stereotypical roles for genders. Some parts of me have been able to experience the freedom of Mumbai whereas other parts of me feel restrained because of the Marwari culture and lived experiences of women in Rajasthan: "What will society think?"

In the words of Virginia Woolf, "My own brain is to me the most unaccountable of machinery, always buzzing, humming, soaring roaring diving, and then buried in mud." However, would Virginia Woolf have felt the same way if she had a room of her own? Perhaps a space to really call her home? Being a strong advocate of women's rights, Virginia Woolf still felt constrained in so many ways. I too felt a certain restraint in my life – it was humming and buzzing until my mind was eventually in the dust. I realized this was not really coming from within me but were voices outside me causing me to feel like that. Was I alone in my experiences? Was I the only one with these voices screaming at me from outside? Surely I was not. There were others. Many others. And I did not even have to search for them. To understand these voices I had internalized, I began a journey towards understanding my Marwari roots in Rajasthan.

To find out the reality of women's lived experiences, I walked streets of villages in Rajasthan, finding myself welcomed into strangers' homes over freshly cooked meals. It was over these meals that women who invited me into their homes also invited me to understand chapters of their life. As an outsider, who looked like a city girl but had roots in Rajasthan and knew almost nobody who had anything in common with them, they saw me as their confidante who they could talk to, share their grievances with and feel lighter for that. They almost treated me like I was between the lines of visibility – I was invisible to them when they wanted to speak their minds, like I was nobody, but I was suddenly visible to them when they wanted to feel heard.

I spoke to some girls from the Marwari community who were as little as six and full of hope for life ahead. I also spoke to Marwari women as old as seventy, sometimes even ninety, who had diverse life experiences and insights about history which they had lived through. Instead of making the project inclusive for only binary women, I also created space to talk to transwomen. I distinctly remember talking to a Marwari woman who was married to a man but was secretly homosexual.

After speaking to a few women, I realized there was a need to turn women's experiences in Rajasthan into a book that is accessible for people globally to understand more about women's struggles and that is how *The Culture Trap* came to be. Culture might empower us but it also traps a lot of us in webs of tradition, culture and heritage. I spoke to over 200 Marwari women in Rajasthan in an attempt to understand my own roots better and that's what led to the creation of this book. The stories I heard broke my heart in ways nobody can imagine. I decided to convert the stories I heard into poems to ease the pain the reader would feel while reading about the painful experiences of these women, twists and turns in their life and also to add an echo effect to the happy stories where the wins and joys experienced by the women are amplified. I thought using poetry would help to get the reader more involved in the cause because in the words of Robert Frost, "Poetry is when an emotion has found its thought and the thought has found words." These poems represent the lived experiences of women who are very much alive and live in Rajasthan. This book is perhaps the first book of its kind – one that uses poetic non-fiction to explain women's struggles.

It was during my conversations with these women that I realized the lines of agency for women in Rajasthan are extremely blurred, specifically because of low levels of literacy and gender inequality they experience since birth. Sexual violence, domestic abuse, female infanticide, female foeticide, denial of right to education, denial of right to speech, denial of right to expression, marital rape and child marriage are all a reality in the state. With this book, I aim to highlight these lived experiences of women and influence change for the better. I hope this book amplifies the voices of the women who have lent their voice to the poems and I also hope you can hear their laughter, hopes, joys, wins, screams, losses, cries and every other emotion in this book. It starts with you.

Thank you for choosing to read this book.

i am born
i open a gift box
it has my childhood
inside
my favourite gift ever
i carry it with me
wherever i go

until one day
the world
snatches it away
from me
before i have even enjoyed
my gift
to the fullest

i once
knitted myself a doll
out of the most beautiful wool
painted red
sourced from my native land

i called the doll
best friend
until one day
her husband beat her up so bad
that she landed in the hospital
then in an asylum
and lost herself forever after that

i am fourteen
snuggling with grandma
the smell of her chiffon saree
crisply draped around her
comforts me

we lie in bed together
and she tells me stories
about how her mother-in-law
suffocated her
without realising that she is
doing the same
to my mother

where does this stop

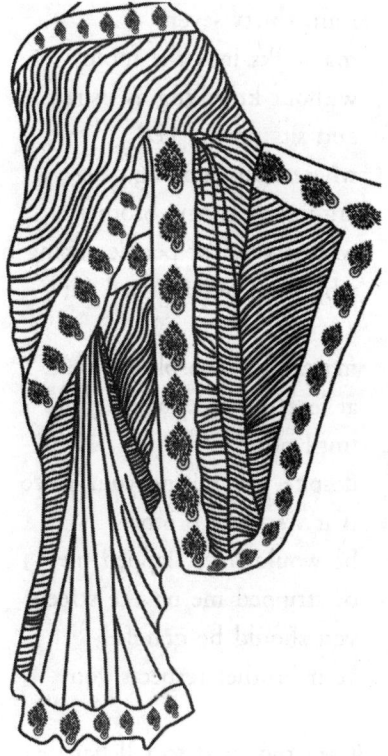

i am thirty-seven
ma walks into the room
without knocking as usual
and sits on my bed
where i am sobbing after
arguing with my brother
who is tired of people asking him
why i am not married yet

ma says to console me
at least he did not hit you
until now
despite you raising your voice
if it were my brother
he would have slapped me
or stripped me on the streets
you should be grateful
your brother respects you

i am too tired to tell her
not being abused
is not a privilege
it is a human right

but i say this to her anyway
not just for me
i say it
because she needs to hear it too

you have only just begun healing
it's a process
more like walking on a path
than climbing a mountain
healing is calm
and serene
and effortless

it will come to you
just give yourself time
and walk on the path every day

i am thirty-six
i walk
with a rucksack on my shoulders
on the snowy grass
around the smell of dewy moonshine
while gazing up at a sky
filled with a million stars
ready to burst open
comets flying across the sky
to make all my wishes come true

i have never felt more gratitude
to be alive
the stars are me
i am the stars
i am the universe in motion
a beautiful language
in which the world communicates

i am alive

why are you offended
when someone calls you a pussy
you should be honored

next time someone says
you are a pussy
in that ugly tone

you say
thank you
with gratitude

i mean
why wouldn't you want to be
a pussy
when
pussy is power

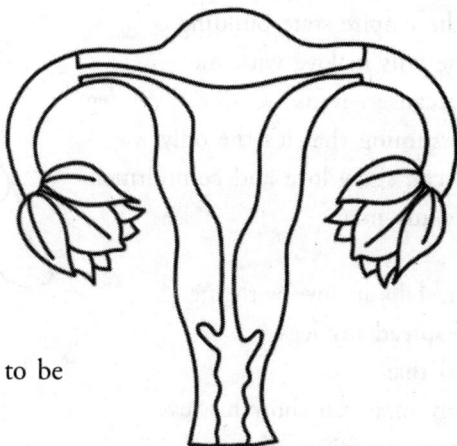

i am forty-six
i meet a man with curly hair
hazel-blue eyes
and fingers as long as
the empire state building
he falls in love with me
because i refuse to spread my legs
assuming that it's the only way
i can show love and commitment
to my man

he falls in love with me
i spread my legs
so that
my man can show his love
and commitment
for me

i like that my sister
read my book

but i don't like
how she called my work
bold
without daring to ask me
if all the traumatic things
i wrote
about my life
were true

i am sixty-nine
ah, a special number
but it has been a while
since i sixty-nined someone
my legs intertwined on his mouth
my mouth intertwined between his legs

but honestly
i feel the same pleasure every day
only because i exist now
more deeply
and aware
than ever

10

never be afraid to speak up
to scream your story out loud
don't be afraid of the consequences
of being heard

when you raise your voice
the injustice of centuries comes to light

much like horror films
you might know if you have watched them
the only way to deal with evil
is to bring it to light

i am forty-seven
standing over the bed
where my ill mother
is unconscious
with all the pills
they fed her
i think about the time
she threw the television remote at my nose
after she walked in on me
exploring myself down there
with my growing fingers
when i was thirteen

i wonder
was it then
i lost some agency
over my own body
when i let my mother command
which parts of myself
i could touch

i shouldn't think about this now
it's not the right time
please don't betray me right now
she is weak and needs my love
not hate
i told my brain

do you really think
there will ever
be a convenient time
for you to think
about things that have given you
panic attacks in the past
my brain asked

the way you used
the word
brave
made me stop
wanting
to ever be
brave

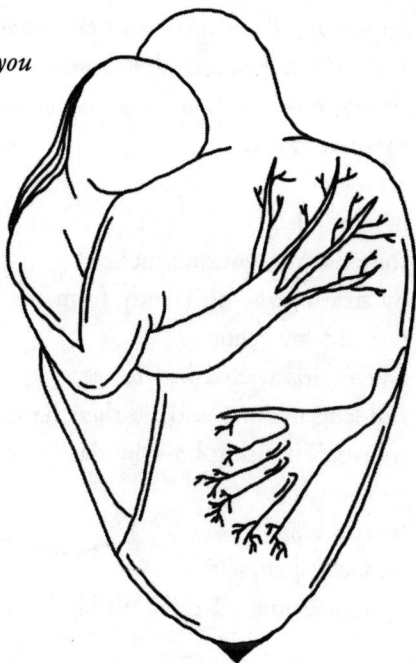

i am forty-eight
i walk into the living room
and hear my parents whispering
do you think her life would be different
if we did not educate her so much
do you think we made a grand mistake
by educating her

first of all
they did not educate me
by treating me differently from my brother
nor did my school
where girls were asked to wear
full-length skirts and tie their hair
to avoid arousing boys in class

first of all
i educated myself
by unlearning all this bullshit

education is what you unlearn

i carry the blood and bones
of all my ancestors who lived before me
i carry something from more than millions of years ago
i carry the gifts of an entire
army across generations within me

and the potential of
generations ahead
who are yet to be born

i am all three at once
the past
the present
the future

i am the product of
a million years of hard work
that my ancestors and the universe put in
and i am the potential creator
of thousands of years ahead
i carry so much within me

but i refuse to carry
the abuse my ancestors went through
i choose to carry
the empowerment they experienced
within me

i am an entire army

i am exactly forty
watching the news where
anchors are discussing
abuse allegations
against the most powerful person
in this world
the president of the united states

i hear a statement
something like
grab 'em by the pussy

i twitch in my seat
what a day for women across the world
cis trans bisexual lesbian black
brown asian hispanic american
everyone

not a very hopeful moment
to be alive

hold leaders
accountable

to everyone out here
who needs to hear this
what happened to you
was never your fault
is still not your fault
and will never be your fault

put an end to self-blame

i am thirty-nine
my friend alleges
i am trying to steal her boyfriend
only because i answered his call
it's basic human decency to answer calls
isn't it

she shames me for being a thief
saying
why don't you meet him alone
set up a date
little does she know
her words sting like poison
choking my ears
making me eyes twitch

why do women trust each other
so little
when we have everything to gain
by trusting more

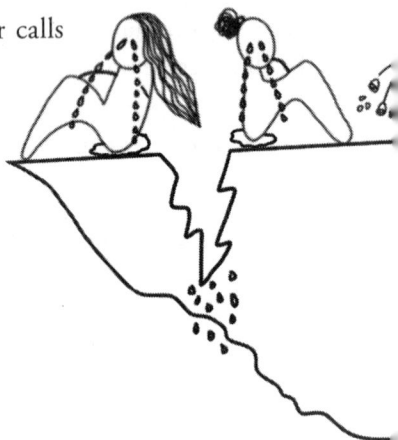

i have a fairly good day
then i find reasons to hate myself
in my own head
sabotaging my own happiness
and peace

i am thirty-eight
it kills me to see
the newborn dog
at my uncle's house is left
with the air conditioner on full
despite the vet's instructions

no air conditioner no fan

thanks to my uncle
who thinks he is an expert at everything
greater thanks to his aging mother
who treats her fifty-year-old son
like a five-year-old baby
mollycoddling him the same way

i hold the puppy
with my own scared hands
for a moment i look into his eyes
and see the same fear
i have felt in the past

i start rubbing his belly slowly
i'm here little one
nothing will happen to you

i am there for him
just like i wish
someone was there for me

animals have rights too

i want to make love
to a man
who will kiss my
stretch marks
moles
and scars
before he kisses my lips

i want to play doctor doctor
with a man
who can inspect me
understand where it hurts
where my insecurities lie
and kiss them out for me

i am forty-one
occasionally i have the sex
with someone other than myself

my family would be petrified
to know i have sex
with people i have no intention
of getting married to
just for fun

but i don't care
what anyone thinks
I'm learning to claim
my own body a little more
as mine
and only mine
every day

i am open to sex
that is
consensual safe and pleasurable
it has to be
all three

they call me brave
and applaud me
for voicing my story out loud

i hope sharing your own story
is a normal act
and not an anomaly
that will be applauded

little do they realise
their applause silences many

while
their silence creates space
for more people to
raise their voice

i am forty-five
thinking about the last man
i dated seriously
more than twenty-five years
ago

he was not the first one
but the last one
who made me feel like
i deserved to be loved less
because i had a past
before him

i refuse to associate with
anyone who does not respect
my history
because history has made me what i am today

if you disrespect my history
you disrespect me

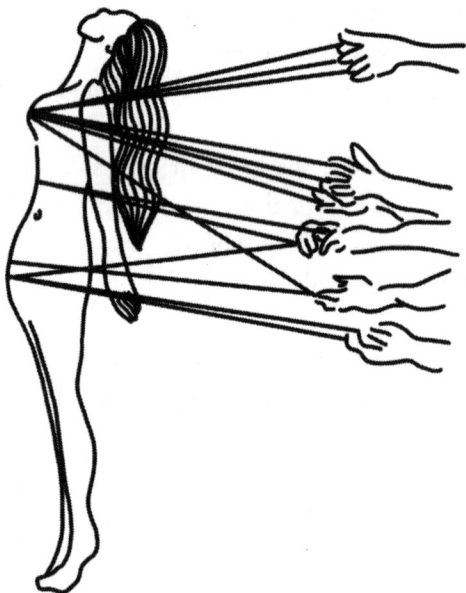

why is it okay
to go to a doctor
when you are hit by a car
and your body bleeds

but it is not okay
to go to a therapist
when life hits you
and your brain bleeds
thoughts you have no control over

i am forty-two
biologically
but still a two-year-old
at using language
while explaining my own abuse
i grow silent
start stammering
shivering

how will i save myself from
future trauma
if i haven't even processed
my past trauma
fully
yet

why do men
care more about
sexual pleasure
than their ability to
give and receive
love

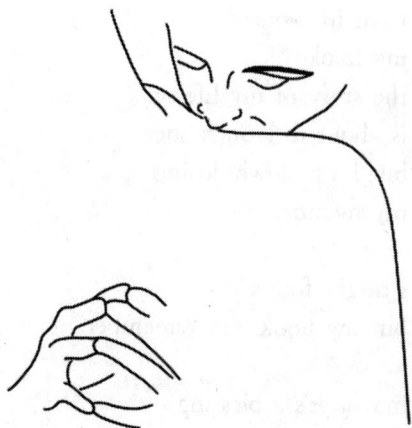

i am fifty-one
my book
the story of my life
is about to launch soon
but i am slowly losing
my memory

i might forget
but my book will remember

maybe it's a blessing
to forget the things that
caused you pain
to dump those memories
swipe them clean

you don't need to remember
you just need to live
and sometimes
forgetting
makes living easy

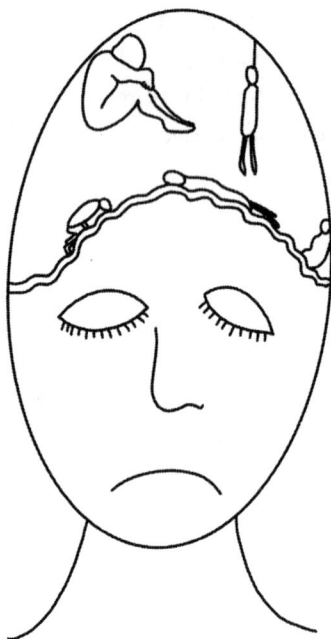

hang in there
don't give up
things are only going to be better
from here

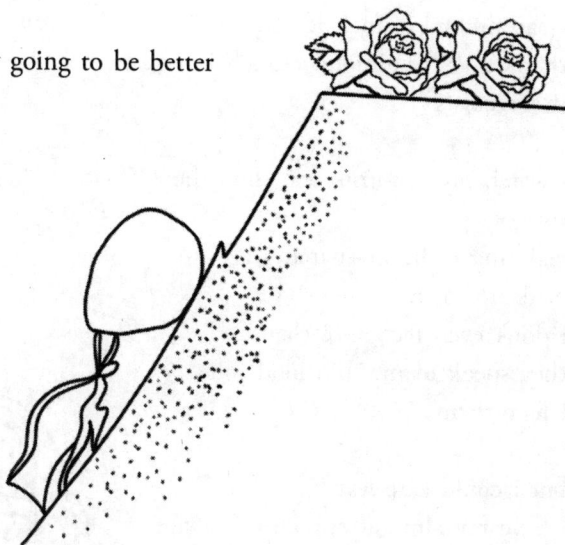

i am fifty-three
i eat almond crunch ice cream
thank god for almond crunch ice cream
if she exists

i watch my favourite television show
two old people
claiming to be my parents
walk up to me
i don't even recognise them
they speak to me in a loud tone
i hate them

but i could care less
i have my almond crunch ice cream
and my favourite television show

life is so good
there is joy in being alive

newness

let me tell you
it was not easy
to stand near my driver's death bed
the same driver who abused me
but i did
and watched
my father and mother cry
unaware about the predator
lying before them

but yes
i celebrated
one less abuser in this world

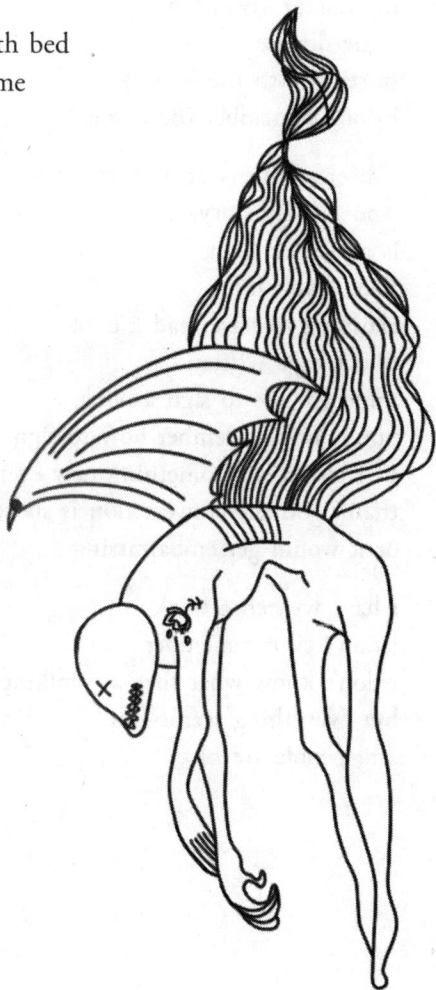

i am fifty-two
my doctor says i have
some disease
starting with the letter a
i don't remember the name

i meet strangers on the streets
who say my story
is also their own
they thank me
claiming to have read a book
that i have written
some ask me to sign a book
but i don't remember how to sign
so i just create something new every time
thank god the conversation is short
or it would get embarrassing

i have written a book
i don't even remember
i don't know what they are talking about
but everything seems fun
and people are nice

sometimes i wonder
if the driver who abused me

also abused
his own daughters

there are six of them
one as young as
five

i am ten
my mother tells me a brutal story
about how her mother
was going to kill her at birth
because she was a girl child
and they did not need any more

you are lucky
we would never think
of doing that
to you
she says

like staying alive
naturally
after being born
is not a basic human right

apparently
in fatehpur
my native village
your gender
determines
your chance at life

let me tell you
it was not easy
to tell the man i loved
and thought was my forever
that i did not want him anymore

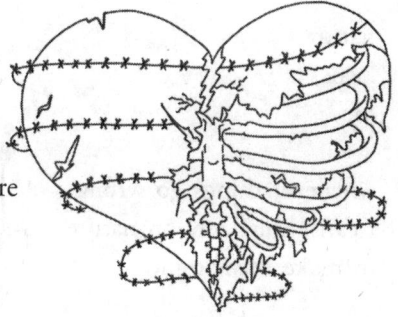

but i did

nature
heals
me

whenever things go wrong
i can always rely on nature
to make them right

walking in the woods
gives me so much
And takes so little

a tree is nothing
but a nut
that stood its ground

i find power within
and heal
thanks to Mother Nature
my beautiful Earth

do you believe in
universal consciousness
see the world around you
you are a part of it
it is a part of you

i am thirty-three
a recurring nightmare
i am inside a room
with all my ancestral women
clad in sarees and pallus
in rajasthan

one was a trans woman
but she wasn't able to tell the
    world that
but she whispers to me
now
save us by saving yourself
and people around you

i look up at the sky
but all i see are dead bodies
corpses hanging from the sky
moaning loudly
like fake orgasms

i wake up

take out your pen
and an empty notebook
and allow yourself
to bleed on that piece of paper

take out an empty canvas
and all shades of paint you own
and pour your heart out
drain it
onto the canvas

this is how healing begins

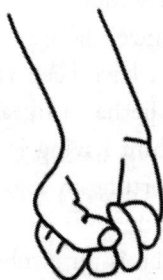

i am forty-four
at my uncle's house
the one i have been visiting since childhood
because he has a likeable personality
despite him having lost
all his fortune in a gambling spree
out of pure ego
i know he is an alcoholic
but i don't think he causes problems

for the first time
i see him overdrink
and scream at his eleven-year-old son
for not being man enough
and getting bullied at school

the eleven-year-old
rushes to the other room crying
while i follow him

he has learned to console himself
he stops crying
and goes about studying
i am a man
i can't cry
he says

as he works silently
but with rage

against his father
which i hope will not
transform into rage
against his wife
later
i can see through
his dramatic silence

i don't write
for the sake of writing
i write
because if i don't
i might stop
living

do something
important
to yourself
to keep yourself sane

water a plant
sketch
dance
sing even if you suck at it
try pole dancing
don't be afraid to look foolish
you might
read a book

hold onto the things
that keep you sane
till your last breath

i am forty-three
i attend my cousin's wedding
where i unsurprisingly hear
my cousin's father has gifted the groom
no less than three cars
jewellery for his mother
gold coins
a fully established business
an expensive suit
a refrigerator
an iPhone
and a couple million rupees

they call it gifts
to make it sound harmless
but we all know
it is just a sinister tradition
carried forward

i think
it's stupid
to start any relationship
with inequality
and expect things
to get better
later

dowry is illegal
maybe gifts should be illegal too

don't let what they think of you change
what you think about yourself
don't let what they think of you change
what you think about yourself
don't let what they think of you change
what you think about yourself
don't let what they think of you change
what you think about yourself
don't let what they think of you change
what you think about yourself
don't let what they think of you change
what you think about yourself
don't let what they think of you change
what you think about yourself
don't let what they think of you change
what you think about yourself

i am eleven
listening to a story
about how my grandmother
cooked food for twenty people
in gigantic silver vessels
every day
after her marriage
spending hours
in the rusted smoky kitchen
in rajasthan
she did it
because she was taught
it's honorable to feed the community
even if it involves
standing in smoke-filled kitchens for
hours
every
single
day

now i see my mother
cooking in the kitchen
for our small family in
mumbai
every day
but she does it because
grandma leaves her
with no choice

i give myself a gift
i open the box
in my room
it's filled with monsters from my past
ones i have buried deep inside me
growing larger and larger
till there is no space
for me to breathe anymore

my therapist asks me
to name each monster
one by one

an unaccepting mother
a sexist father
an abusive childhood
a broken nose
no claim over my own body
discrimination from my brother
lack of solidarity
toxic boys at school
insecure girlfriends

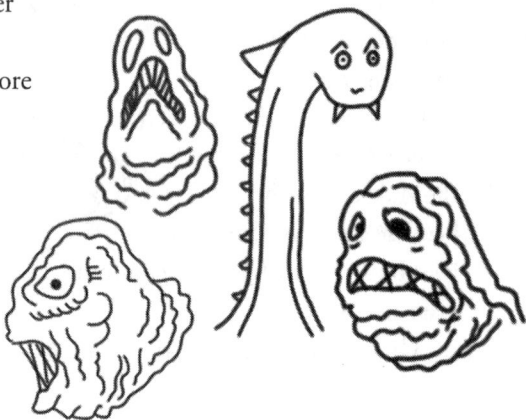

i keep naming the monsters
one by one
and they grow smaller

i am ten
i don't understand
why my mother walked in
and turned off the television
and slapped me across my face
when i was watching a pole dancing show
america's best pole dancer
i wish i could move my body like that

this show isn't for women or girls
don't watch stuff meant for boys and men
she said

i really don't understand
if dancing is an art
i can learn at school
why is pole dancing not an art too

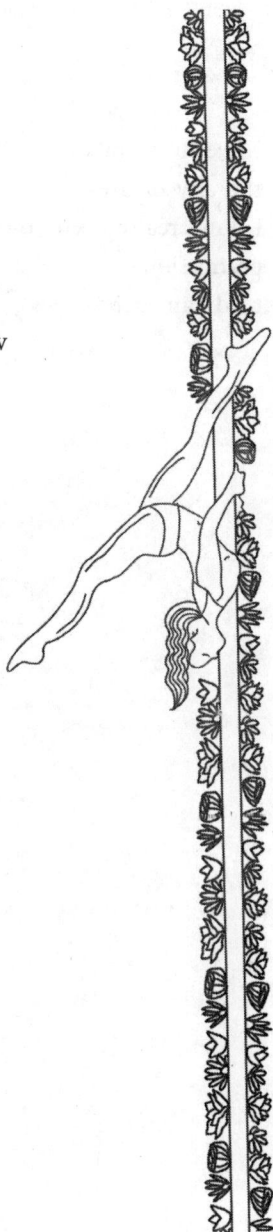

i live in mumbai
the city of dreams
i don't really need your
permission
to dream here

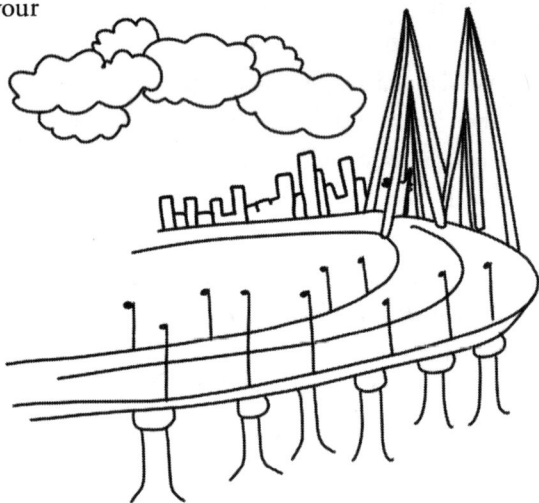

i am twelve
as usual grandma is telling me stories
about fatehpur
she tells me
it's common for a sixteen-year-old girl
to marry a sixty-year-old man
if he is rich enough
in fatehpur
and other parts of rajasthan

it's not legal
but apparently
people still do it

i think i have daddy issues
because of grandma

my family moved from
fatehpur
a village in rajasthan
to mumbai
some generations back

but somehow
they still think
like most people there
even now

where the virtue of a woman
starts and ends
with her sense of shame
towards her own body

i am fifteen
its diwali
the hindu festival of lights
the sky is lit with
ecstatic firecrackers
bursting open in different colours

dada my grandfather
lights the firecrackers
but dadi
my grandma
sits inside the house
with her pallu
unable to see the fireworks
burst in the sky

i dislike diwali a little after that
how can we celebrate
when women cannot enjoy
the festival
to the fullest

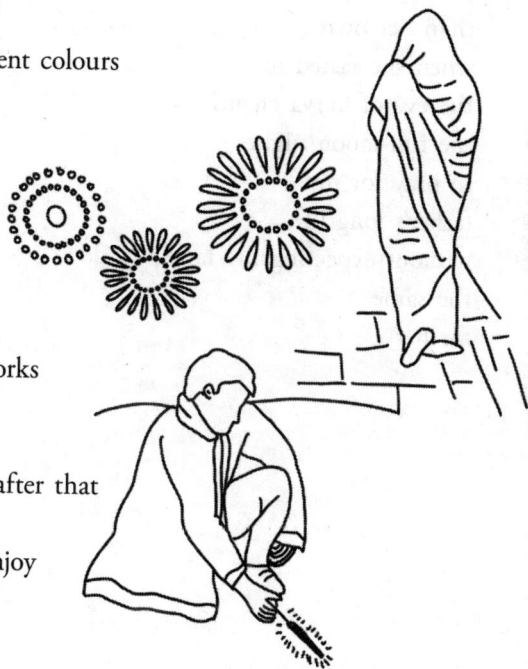

i first realised
that my mother
treated my father's life
as more valuable
than her own
when she fasted on
the eve of karva chauth
the full-moon night
to pray for my
father's long life
without expecting my father to do
the same
for her

don't believe
everything you see
don't believe
everything you hear
believe
everything you smell
because your instinct is so sharp
that you can smell things
from miles away

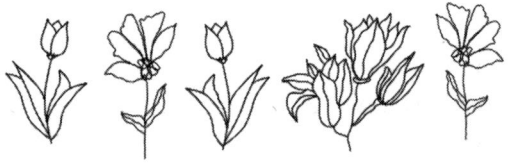

things are slowly working in your
favour
even if it feels like
they are not

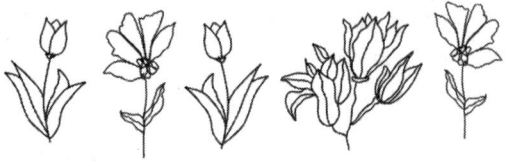

and
why do you allow yourself
to look sad
when you can just walk
to the closest mirror
and see
triumph
written all over your
face

you know
something is wrong
with society
when it is easier to publish
your own story
anonymously
than to claim it
as your own

fatehpur
from where my roots are
why do they call
a girls marriage
kanyadaan
literally meaning
donation of the girl child

are women objects
that can be donated or discarded
at their family's whims

can someone stick a banner
saying
objects are donated
women are not
because people still need
to hear this

how do you expect
to see equality
when the language around women
is so messed up

why are wives expected to
fast
to gain a long life
for their husbands
when some of their lives
would be better off
without them

mental health is not a choice
stop blaming people for being depressed
mental health is a state of being
can you choose to not have cancer
mental health is somewhat like that

yes you might avoid smoking
if you don't want cancer
but some people who never smoked
suffer with cancer too
you can't just choose to not have cancer

if you can go to a doctor to cure cancer
why can't you go to a therapist
for your mental health

i am kind
but not the same kind as childhood
not everyone deserves my kindness

my kindness is only for those
who are willing to earn it
and for those
who have not been indifferent
when they could make my
life better

i am that childhood art trick
where all colours you can ever imagine
are crayoned on a canvas
the blues the greens the reds
the oranges the yellows the whites
the flowery lavenders the dark browns

then black is crayoned over
all the other colours
and finally scratched to expose the surface
where you can see all the real artwork

have you realised
you find the best things
in places you never imagined
the ones that looked black and rusty
but possessed so much colour within

serendipity

life is not a punching bag
life is a process
of slowly
breathing in and breathing out

breathe in

                                        breathe out

breathe in

                                        breathe out

breathe in

                                        breathe out

breathe in

                                        breathe out

observe
everything around you
closely

you are a spectacle of life

why is it easier
to cling to life
when you are about to die
than to live fully
when you are not

my healing has begun
i acknowledge i was abused
but i don't have to stay that way
my abuse
was my past
my empowerment
is my present
and future

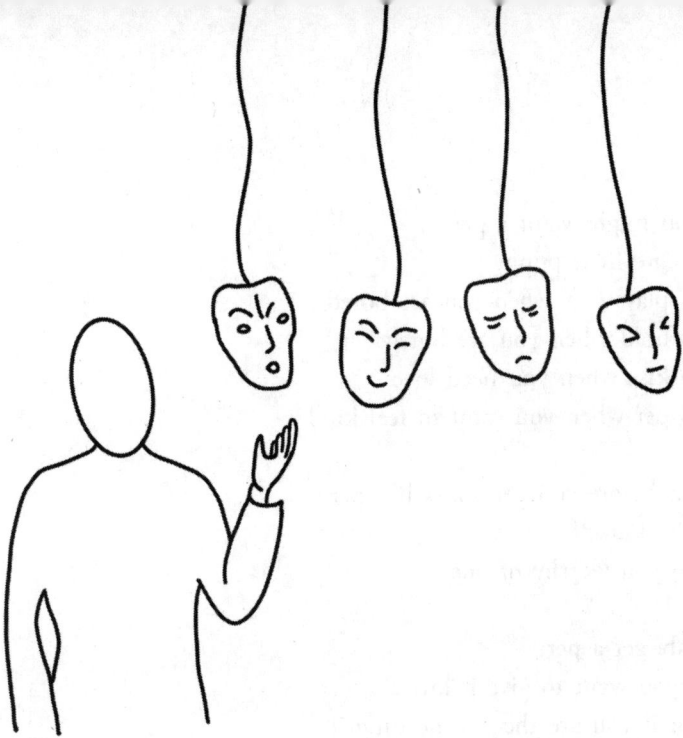

why is it
looked down upon
to make love
to your brother's best friend
when it's consensual

but acceptable to get raped
by your husband
after marriage

you might want a pet
a cute little puppy
to play with when you are bored
to hold when you are lonely
to kiss when you need love
to pet when you want to feel kind

but before you get yourself a pet
ask yourself
are you worthy of one

only get a pet
if you want to give it love
not if you are the one needing it

a pet is not your toy
it's like a little baby
demanding your commitment

i have been
abused
but i am not
an abuser
the chain has to stop
with someone

being subjected to abuse
even if as a spectator
is abuse
in itself

why is it surprising
my brother and i don't get well along
we fight a losing battle against
discrimination in our homes
and from everyone else in society

with me on the frontlines more often than him
he has little reason to fight
the liberties are in his favour
and he is unaware
about the price he pays
for liberties that are his

like fighting for his sister
is not enough reason
like i don't tie a rakhi to him
every year
hoping he will do more

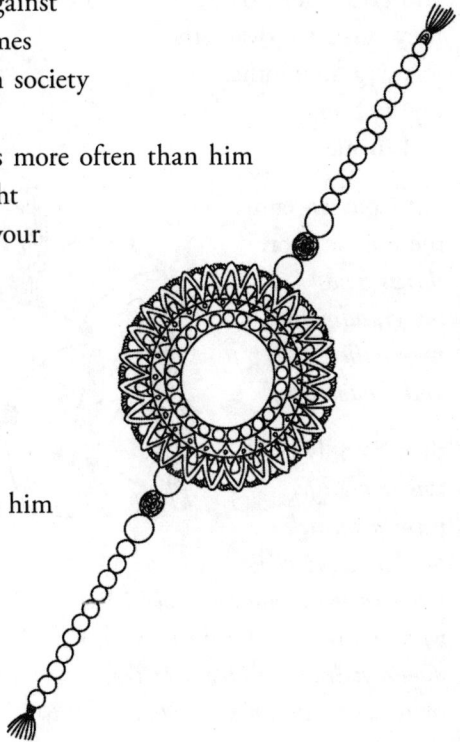

my great grandmother was abused
just like her great grandmother
just like her great grandmother
just like her great grandmother
and generations of women before her
they carried forward the abuse
to my grandmother
my mother
and to me

but i put an end to it
there is no more
this is how
my grandmother lived
my mother lived
and i have lived

there is only
this is my life
i am a miracle
my life is my choice
i can carve it into whatever i like
paint it with my favourite colours
mould it into my favourite shape
compose it into an individual melody

to bring change you need to be the change

and when exactly
did you begin to understand
you were abused
not loved

my mental health
is much better
now that i am
prioritising myself

embrace yourself
in your favourite quilt
with a hot mug of latte
treat yourself with expensive sushi
watch your favourite movie
call your best friend
or your therapist
buy that plane ticket
tell them you love them
call your parents
write that book
rise in love
float in the sky

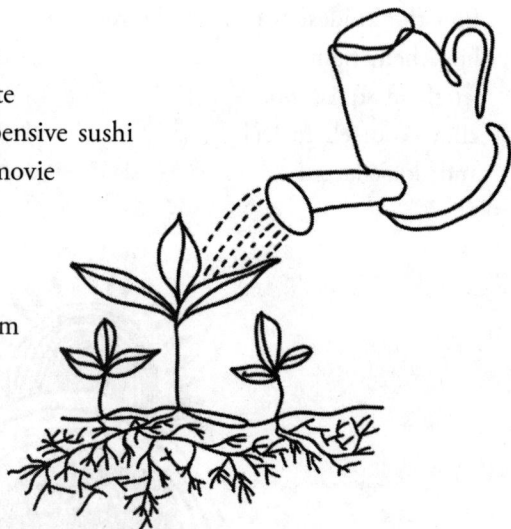

this is your sign
to embrace yourself

find the kindest person in the room
hug them tight
let them squish you
allow yourself to feel
and don't let go

walk to your kitchen now
find your favourite mug
boil some water on the flame
melt dark chocolate
as much as you like
add hot milk
almond milk works if you are vegan
cinnamon
honey drops
smell the infusion
soak it into you
let the heavenly smell engulf you

you have been through so much
little one
you deserve it

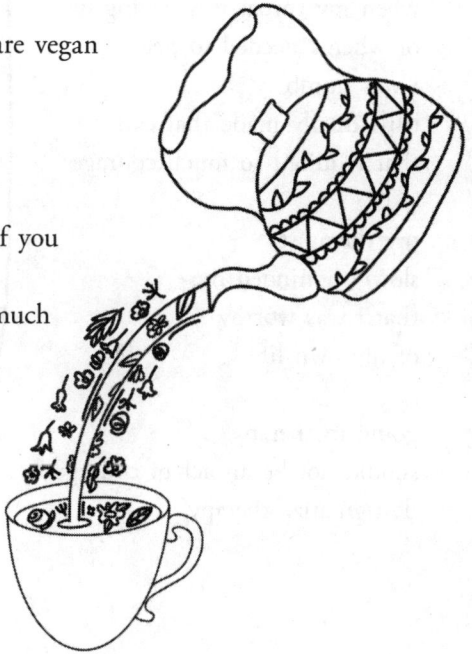

i was afraid of therapy
i was afraid of being called mad
i couldn't tell anyone i needed therapy
until things got so bad
i couldn't get up from bed
when my throat was drying up
or when i needed to pee
i was numb
till i finally made that call
that required so much courage

my therapist
slowly reminded me
that i was worthy
of my own life

going to therapy
should not be an act of courage
destigmatize therapy

my grandmother was taught
when you get married
keep your eyes lowered
to respect others

i taught myself
look at the world
straight in the eye
to respect myself

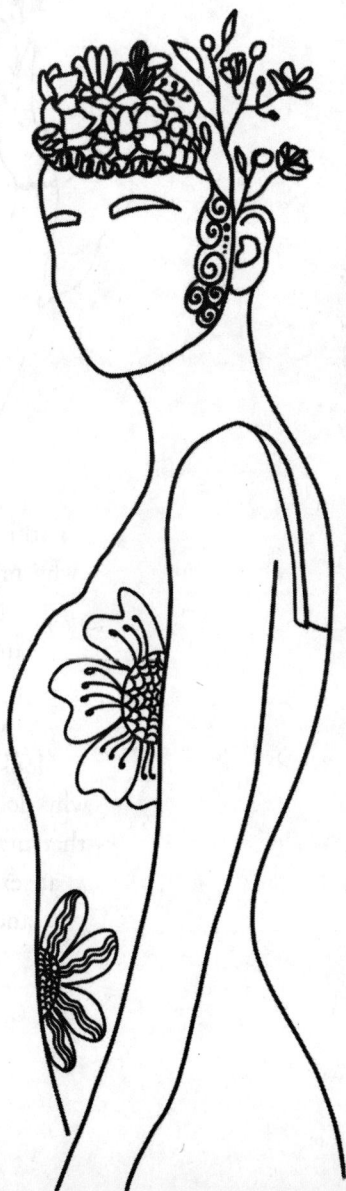

i still don't understand
why my brother's success
is celebrated
and encouraged

while mine is
looked down upon
why do some people think
that my success will bring
an expense to my life
and will cost me
dearly

it saddens me to know
that sometimes
children can be abused
as soon as they are born
punished with death
only because of their gender

i refuse to accept
traditions
that teach my grandma
to sit on the floor
while my grandfather
sits on the couch

or ones where a woman
is expected to begin eating
only when her husband
is done
feasting

i am here
to bring the goddamn system down
and to create
traditions
of my own
for all of us
out here

you
are
capable
of
being
patient
and
savouring
every
moment

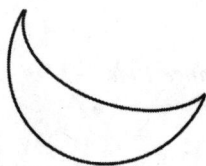

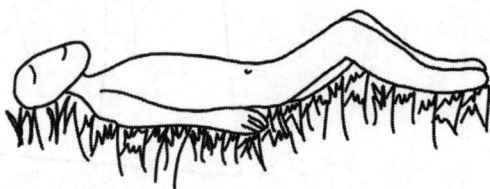

i stand in front
of the mirror
completely naked
and touch
each scar
on my body
and
slowly whisper
to myself

i have lived through this
i will continue living despite this
i love myself and nothing will change that

i give each scar
the attention
and love
it deserves

how will we change
anything
if you keep reminding me
what it is
instead of focusing on
what it could be

sometimes when i sit
on my desk and write
i forget that i am human
i get lost in my thoughts
my hands move on their own
my pen brain heart and hand
are one
i flow on paper
seamlessly

calm and steady flow state

uphold
your lover
to the same standards
you uphold
your closest friends

to avoid
using others
as a means of
escape

embrace your solitude

if you embrace
patriarchy
you surrender
your longing
to love

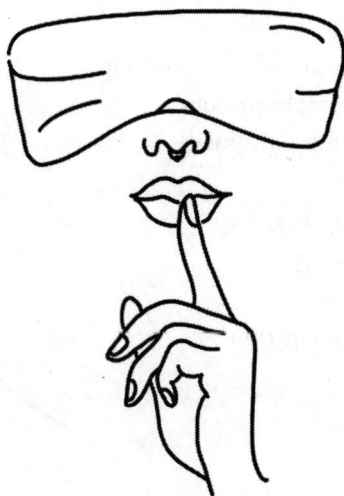

to build
a healthy relationship
emphasize on
mutual growth

rather than
duty
or
obligation

every time we speak
we have the power
to radically transform
the world
we live in

how can i expect
you to stay the same
when i can't even relate
to the person i was
back in january
now in march
the same year

same take a day to grow
some take months
some a year
take your time

it is okay
to outgrow them

you are a hydrangea
born to bloom
into the awe-inspiring existence
that you already are

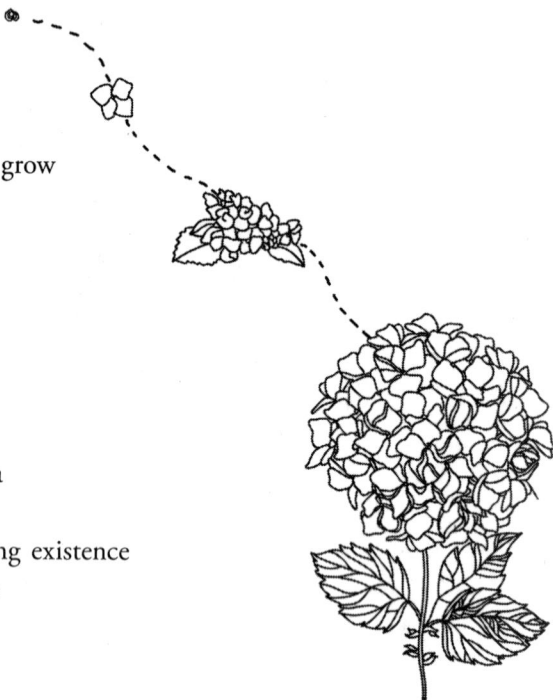

*t*o learn
self-love
one must first
overcome
low self-esteem

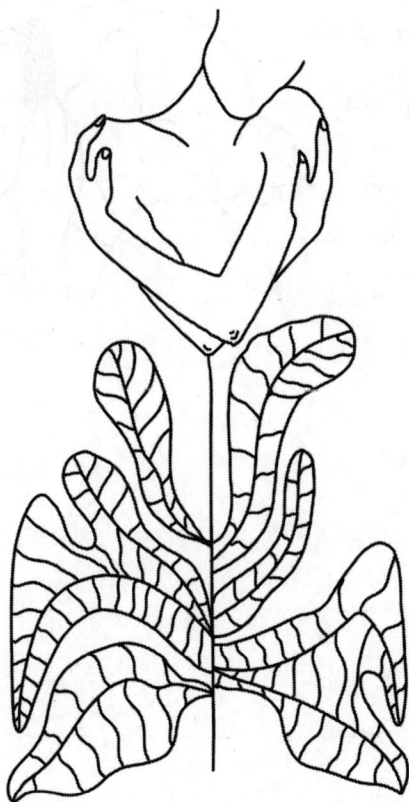

it is not surprising
that women have traditionally
been accused
of gossiping

gossiping has often been
the only social interaction
where women felt comfortable
to express their opinions
and talk about
how they really feel

why women gossip

talk
to
your
community
and
highlight
their
struggles
over
their
achievements
to
build
a
better
tomorrow

you are the future

my family
threw a party
and distributed gifts
when my brother
was born

but i was
greeted with
silence
at my birth

should i be sorry
for not giving
trigger warnings
in my book

how could i give
trigger warnings
when abuse is
so deeply normalised
in my life

i hope when
this year ends
you find the courage
to say
thank you
before
i hope next year is better

thank you

i think
my mother
grandmother
sister
best friend
and many other women
would have
significantly different lives
if they were
financially independent

i just want
someone to hold me
close and tight
and whisper softly in
my ear
i am here to stay
i am here to stay
i am here to stay
i am here to stay
i am here to stay
i am here to stay
i am here to stay
i am here to stay
till i calm down

why do i feel
like an imposter
while writing my own story
surely there are people
with greater struggles
and more suffering
than me

and then
i remind myself
struggle and suffering
are measured in existence
not in depth

how does one measure
who has suffered more

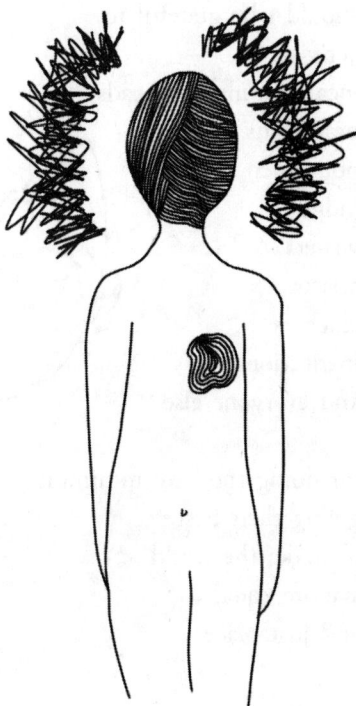

should i be grateful to
activists
local community heads
politicians
policemen
judges
writers
artists
teachers
institutions
and everyone else

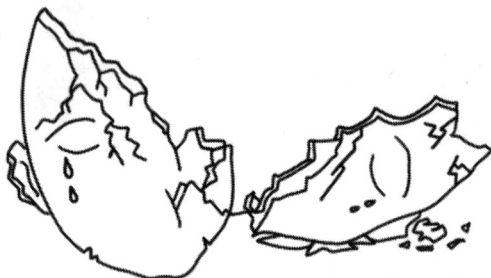

for doing the bare minimum
giving their best
to make the world
a more equal
and just place

i know
there is no need
for me to be
but i am

have you ever played
with lego blocks
the ones you stack
on top of each other `
to make something bigger

it only makes sense
when the full stacking
pieces put together
one by one
is complete

life is a lot
like lego blocks

i don't know
what you should do
but i know what you should not

1. don't give up on yourself
    life is a beautiful solo performance
    with dim orchestra music
    playing in the background

2. don't stop trying to make
    peace with your past
    even if it was traumatic

3. don't expect anyone but
    yourself to be there
    for you

4. never be afraid to raise your voice
    when you are uncomfortable even
    if the source of discomfort
    is your own mind

5. never make the space around you smaller
    to accommodate someone
    who is demanding
    the box around you needs growth
    stop trying to fit into boxes
    you know you have overgrown

TO DO LIST

☑ Be kind to yourself
☑ smile more 😊
☑ Live and let live
☑ Not have regrets
☑ Stay beautiful

6. never not dissociate with someone
    who is mentally emotionally or physically abusive

7. never settle for anyone who makes
    you feel any less than an absolute
    sparkling diva of a human being

8. stop trying to find chronology
    try to find beauty in irregularity

9. stop looking back
    unless to see how far you have come

10. don't let someone else
    no matter how much you think
    you love them
    choose anything for you
    even if it's your favourite flavour of ice cream

11. stop trying to base your standards
    on the experiences
    of someone you have known
    just because your mother was in an abusive relationship
    with your father
    you don't need to settle for non-abusive
    instead of healthy
    supportive
    and loving

12. don't hide your story
    from a stranger
    just because you meet someone on the subway
    for fifteen minutes
    it does not mean
    that you cannot change their life

13. don't forget to live
    in the moment
    while focusing on the future
    time is just a whimsical singer
    moves slow or fast
    based on its own personal mood

14. don't be afraid or ashamed
    of your own identity
    even if it offends someone else
    their opinion is none of your business
    you have nothing to gain or lose
    from what they think about you

my father collects
all the pages of my manuscript
scattered across my writing desk
and says
i will kill myself
if you ever publish this
but i defy him anyway
so that it's easier
for everyone on the same boat
after me
i hope there are none

solidarity between sisters is empowering
i don't know how I could have done
anything without her
the way my sister looks at me
tells me she believes in me

she is
powerful
intelligent
kind
beautiful

she makes me feel
powerful
intelligent
kind
beautiful

we all deserve to feel that way

i am fifty
crinkled eyes and wrinkled face
only more confident in my stride than eve
ready to take over the world
with my writing
i sit on a table
and start penning down everything
furiously
so that people know my story
understand they are not alone
fighting for basic rights
standing up for themselves
against generations of injustice

i know it will take years
to bring change
to live equally
but i also know
that more of us will march there together

why do mothers
police what their own daughters wear

having given birth to their daughters
stark naked from their own womb
shouldn't mothers be the first to stand
for their daughters' freedom

or does gender change
the mother's right to stand up
for her own child

i am thirty-three
i have three things
to say to you
which will change the course
of your life

1. don't let anyone tell you
   you are worth less
   than you believe you are

2. set boundaries
   or you might lose agency
   in places you need it most

3. love yourself
   because you are capable of more love
   than anyone else can offer
   to you

my mother did not give birth to me
she ate me up
like the morning-after pill
with an ounce of bitterness
kept me in her belly for nine months
till i fought my way out of there
without being strangled
and shat me outside her vagina

she treated me like i wasn't a blessing
but a curse
that could be discarded

i am thirty-four
my father walks into my room
without knocking
guess some things never change

he draws up the courage hesitantly
to ask me
without looking into my eyes
do you have a thing for other women

the word lesbian lingers in the air
around us
like an allegation
only because i choose to
stay unmarried

i look straight into his eyes
and say
i am not single
i am complete
just the way i am
i came into this world
from my mother's womb
dripping in her blood
without any notion
of needing anyone else
and that's how i will leave

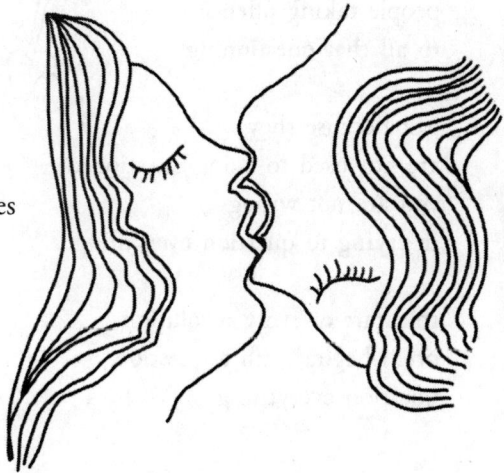

the only person i really have a thing for
is
myself

don't assume things
always ask questions
to understand
what people mean
when they say things
if you don't ask questions
you will never know

don't be afraid of
people taking offence
to all that questioning

just because they
are not used to being questioned
you are not wrong
in trying to question everything

the start of every revolution
often begins with a question
question everything

i am thirty-five
my illusion breaks
when i realize that my girl best friend
does not really deserve to be
my best friend

she comes to me crying
telling me grim tales about
how her husband beats her up
only occasionally
not hard enough for her to land
in the local hospital
unlike her other married friends
at least there was no blood
only cuts
she says

i have known her since i was five
but i don't need a friend
who can't be a friend
to herself
first

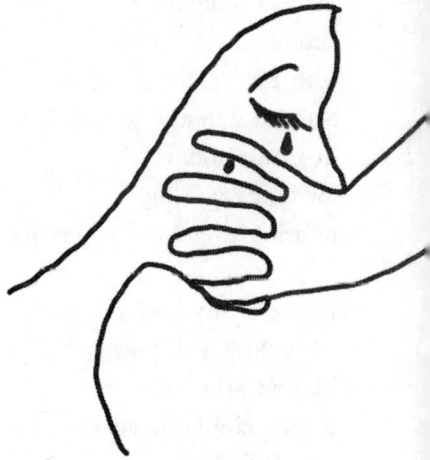

make friends with people who have befriended themselves

my parents think
there is something
wrong
with me
because i choose to
sit in my room
for hours writing
refusing to get out of my pajamas

i stare at my books
with sheer will power
like no other woman
in our family dared to
ever before

little do they know
there is nothing wrong with me
i am setting the course right
for generations of women after me

i am thirteen
when i see the first bloody sight
of my leaking vagina
i rush and tell my mother
my stomach hurts
i think i'm about to die
or maybe i'm cursed
mother looks at me with pity
rather than celebration
she knows
the ability to reproduce
never created a favorable situation
for a woman in a traditional marwari household

ma does not end the cycle
either

115

i don't tell my father
about my childhood abuse
he is a kind honest and generous man
telling him how the world
has not been kind to me
will be the same as
robbing him a little bit
of his kindness

i am not a thief

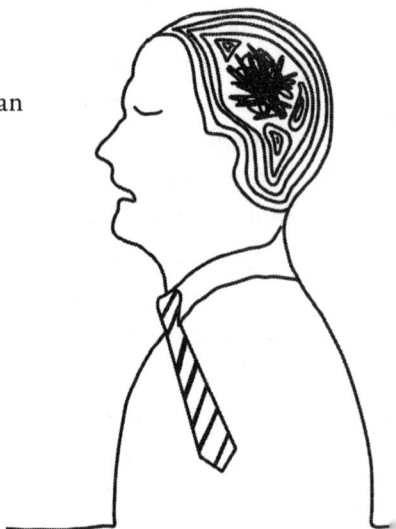

i am thirty-three
dancing with the man
of my dreams
in a room flooded with moonlight
a special orchestra playing just for us
with roses in my hair
hearts in my eyes
until the man of my dreams disappears
right before the song climaxes
leaving me with his silhouette
and sharp memories about the time
when he chose to stay

stay a little longer will you

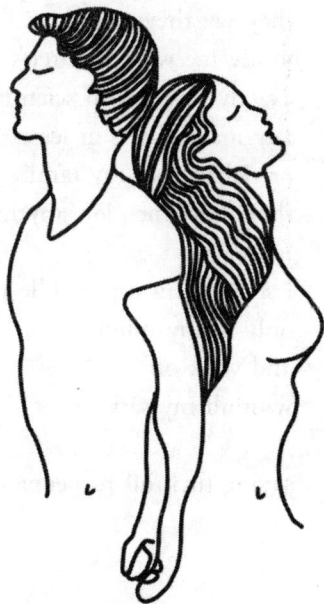

they say they can't wait
to see me in a red ghaghra
clad in diamond jewellery
a mantika on my head
necklace flowing till my abdomen
mehendi from my fingertips
all the way till my elbow
and on my feet all the way up
till my knees

they say they can't wait
to see me walk in circles
exactly seven crisp scientific rounds with a man
any man who is at least rich enough
or richer than my family
they don't mention anything about love

i show them my middle finger
only in my mind
and walk off
with all my sass

saying fuck off to people mentally can bring you peace

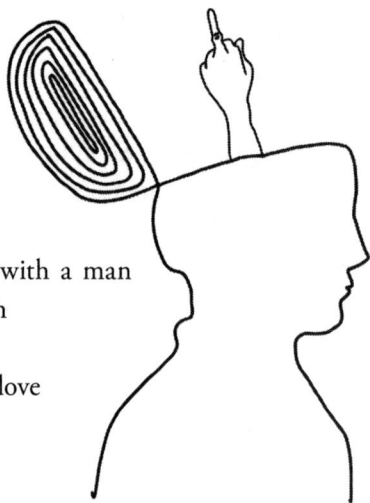

i am thirty
as a journalist
i have spent my entire life
chasing facts and truth
yet i have found
only three deep truths about my own life

1. my most important relationship
    is with myself

2. i need to love myself
    in greater magnitude
    every single day

3. nothing and no one
    are worth more
    than my self-respect

i have spent thirty years
of my life
to come to terms
with these
three basic truths

my sister thinks
i am bipolar
she thinks
i am like a pendulum
swinging from one side to another
crazy happy at one point
drowning in my own tears the next
there is no balance

ask me what it's like
i am bipolar

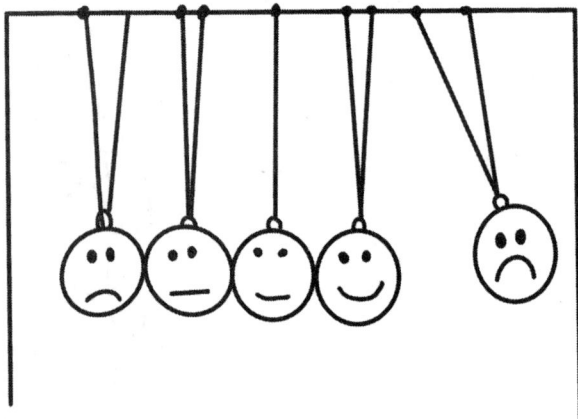

i am twenty-six
i write articles about
feminism
gender equality
sexuality
touching personal topics like
abuse harassment and sexism
i listen to others stories
about loss of agency in their lives
childhood trauma
and also know that it is my own
but i never tell them that
there is a strange twisted solace
in knowing

i am not alone

are you really comforted by the thought
that you are not alone
or do you know
there is no comfort in that

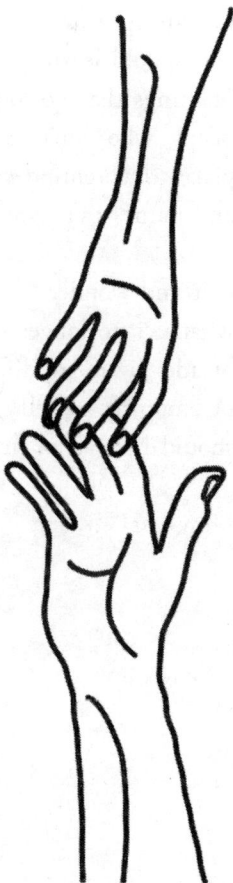

my therapist says
you should learn to let go
of things that no longer serve you
people who don't add joy to your life
places that remind you of abuse
and names that don't empower you

i sit and wonder
what if i no longer serve myself
or add joy to my life
or empower myself
should i let go of myself too

i am lost

i am twenty-one
dada my grandfather
has passed away
dadi my grandma
is beating her chest
crying out loud
and begging father
to burn her alive on the same pyre as dada
she says
how can i live when my beloved is dead
what now is my purpose in life

she was taught that the will to die for her husband
was an act of dedication
little did she understand
that dying for someone else
was self-abuse

why are women raised with such little
sense of self
where their idea of live starts
with family
and ends at
her husband

sometimes the silence in my mind
is louder and darker than
the voice in my head

i can reason with the voice in my head
but the silence is diabolic
it catches hold of me from behind
and throws me off the cliff

does silence scare you too

i am twenty-four
looking at my own majestic and dreamy eyes in the mirror
as i vow to cross my heart
and never get married
to anyone but myself
i know that it is an injustice
to commit to love someone else
when i struggle to love myself every day
the way i deserve self-love
or even accept myself
for what i truly am

can you love someone else till you love yourself the way you
deserve to be loved

Only a fool would be patient when the moment is right.
Isn't it?

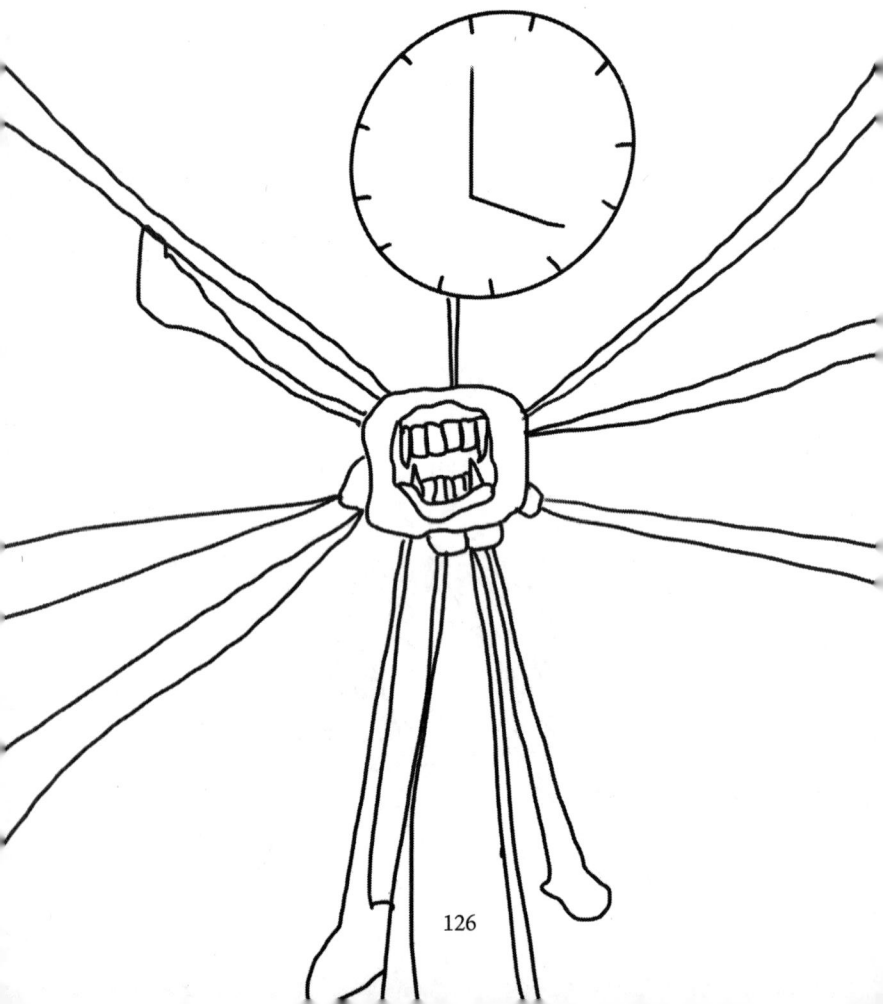

i am twenty-five
let me tell you how i feel
about my unaware father
paying for an angioplasty
a heart surgery
for the same heartless driver
who watched rape porn on the loudspeaker
and felt me up my school uniform

let me tell you how i feel
about my father
spending our savings
to save the man
i had to save my childhood self from

i am trying to tell you how i feel
but i can't

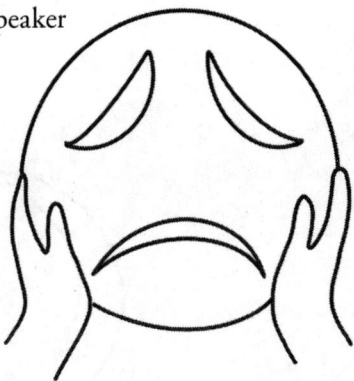

First wait for the right person.
Then wait for the right moment.
Then for the right person with the right moment.

i am fifteen
sitting on a chair
near my first-ever boyfriend
in an otherwise empty classroom
way after school hours

he looks at my developing breast
and asks
aren't they supposed to be bigger
like sexy women i watch in porn

i do not have the heart to tell him
that his dick is smaller
than the men i have watched
because deep down i know

size doesn't matter
the person does

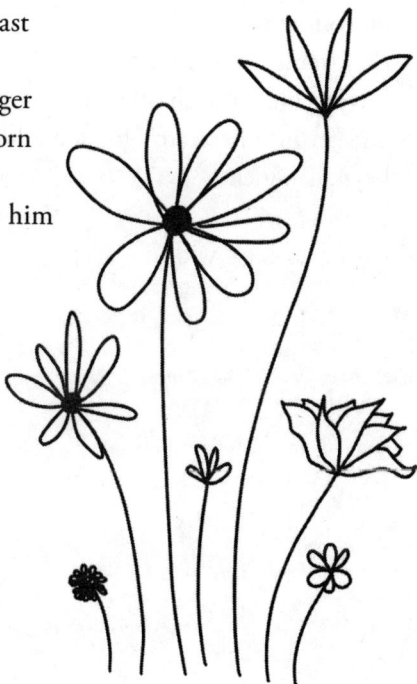

i think
i am subconsciously designed to choose men
who disappear on me
after promising me the world
and making me believe i have it all
they act like i am their everything
but one fine day
they vanish into thin air
leaving me with ghastly stinging memories
and an infinite search for something
beyond myself

i need to look within

i am eighteen
in my dorm room
with my boyfriend
naked by his side
surrounded by the smell of sex
while i whisper a secret in his ear
i was abused as a child
seeking his acceptance
i say right before he gathers his clothes
and walks out of the room

in that moment
i know i might never find acceptance
in anyone else
but i shall always seek it
within

i am twenty-three
walking on the beach
in an attention-seeking neon-yellow bikini
when i observe my own mother
the woman who spat me outside her vagina
when i was stark naked
covered in her body juice
looking at my brown nudity
with shame
as she averts her eyes
at my defiance
to wear something sober

i refuse to wear anything
anyone expects me to
i embrace my brown nude body
with all its imperfections
and give myself a tight hug
as the salty wild waves crash at my feet

If you want to make someone stop doing something, say it as an instruction.

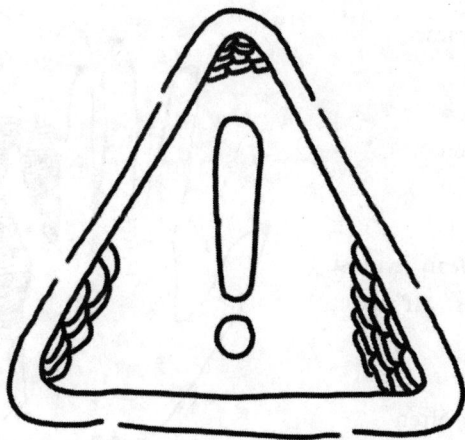

i am thirteen
i will remember
this year
for the rest of my life
the driver
the predator
tried to touch me

squeeze my thigh
when i drew
the courage
swelling inside me
to say no
for the first time
in years

that was when
i realised
saying no
when you mean it most
is the greatest act of
self-defence

say no more often

134

you need to stop making
a man
your priority
the moment he is kind
or better than toxic
or unabusive towards you

i know that you hold onto
your past trauma
so that no one can hurt you
the way he did

wake up
you are one full divine glass of wine yourself
you don't need water to fill you

when you are all you need
pure divinity

i am eleven
my great grandmother
gave birth to exactly
the same number of children
eleven

ten girls back to back
stopping only after
the eleventh child
a boy
was finally born

she loved each girl
in descending order
of birth
each girl child
a greater burden than
the previous one

my grandfather was loved
the most
because he restored
her honour
as a woman
in the family

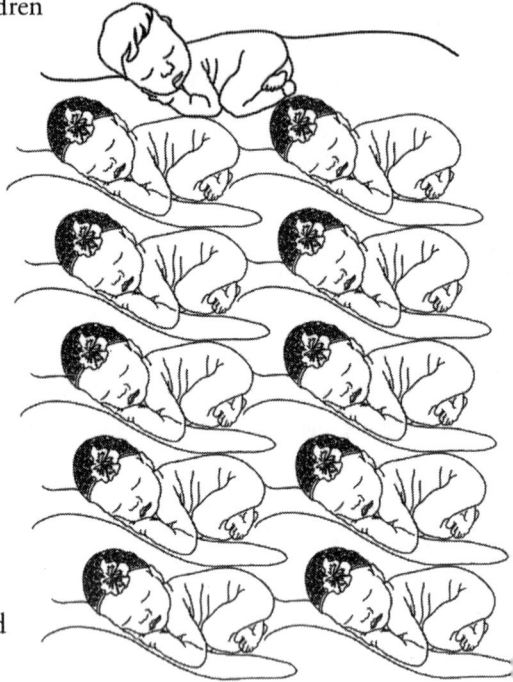

If someone makes you happy in your imagination, they're enough.

i am five
my hungry belly controls me
i am on the lookout for food in the kitchen
where grandma is hurling abuses
at the fourteen-year-old
unschooled boy working at home
she picks up her slipper
and aims it at his face
i freeze
but force my legs to run away
hungry no more

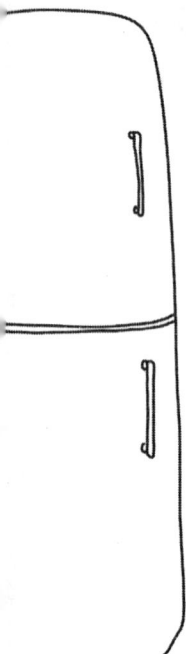

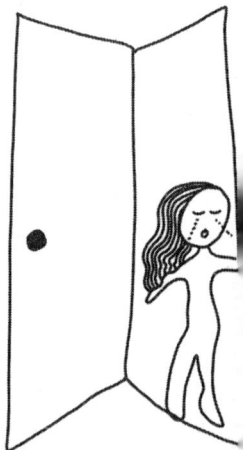

I already have everything I need.

i am seven
i watch my father slap my mother
now six months pregnant
with my baby brother
yes they asked the doctor the gender
willing to drop the baby if it was a second girl
he slaps her over and over again
for raising her voice over his
i want to scream
ssstooooppppp
but the words don't come out
i shiver
and wonder
can the unborn brother sense the abuse too?
i feel solidarity with him before he is even born

Be happy in the present, imagining yourself happy in the future will only make you unhappy in the present.

i am eight
back in the car after school
with the same family driver
in my school uniform
a longish pleated skirt
and a white full-sleeved top
covering every inch of my body
obviously without a bra
eight-year-olds don't wear bras
when my driver
assumes the liberty
to linger his index finger
on my undeveloped juvenile chest
and says
let's play hide and seek in the car
with a devilish smile

I ran and stumbled,
hence I need to go hand in hand.

i am nine
out for a sleepover at my aunt's
who is alone at home
while her husband is out for a so-called
business trip
really just fucking other women in bar bathrooms

she kisses me wet
on my lips and tongue and chest
leaving me utterly confused
but i like the tingling sensation
but it still feels wrong

i go home and confide in my mother
who laughs at me and says
i'm sure she kissed your cheek
so confident when she wasn't even there

i tell my cousin
who believes me
unlike my mother
because he too has been through
   the same thing
kissed and touched in places
without his consent

young solidarity

I want everything all at once. Why?

i am thirty-two
i might look harmless
but i am
googling and finding ways to kill myself

surely there must be
a cure for loneliness
i don't find anything
i have not already tried before
except jumping off
a fifty-one-storey building

i stand on the ledge
willing to put an end
to my misery
but i step back hastily
for i have not changed the world yet
in my own little way

maybe i suffer
so that others won't have to
maybe it will lead to something good

i have to create some meaning
out of my suffering
or i might kill myself
next time

i did not suffer for nothing

Being connected to past pain is the only way forward

i am thirty-one
when i light two cigarettes
and put them between my lips together
inhaling the bitter-sweet smoke
deep inside my lungs
with little regard for my life

i don't care if i die
better now than later

smoking makes me feel more alive
even if it's only for three minutes

there is nothing glorious about self-abuse

The issue with me is
I can express anger more easily than love.

i am twenty
i hear my uncle
a father figure in my life
brag about blowing thousands of rupees
in a dance bar
while his eleven-year-old daughter
eats on the dinner table
eavesdropping on stories about
her father's misadventures
in silence
but not ease

i imagine countless women
sitting on the table in silence
often with pallus covering their face
unable to speak up
or to create solidarity

i break the chain
i voice my opinion
out loud
despite the consequences
i know i will have to face

rather face consequences than be silent

why is it
something like
men
women
gay
bisexual
lesbian
trans
intersex
pansexual
androgynous
asexual
and the list goes on

than simply
all of them
on the same line
in no particular order

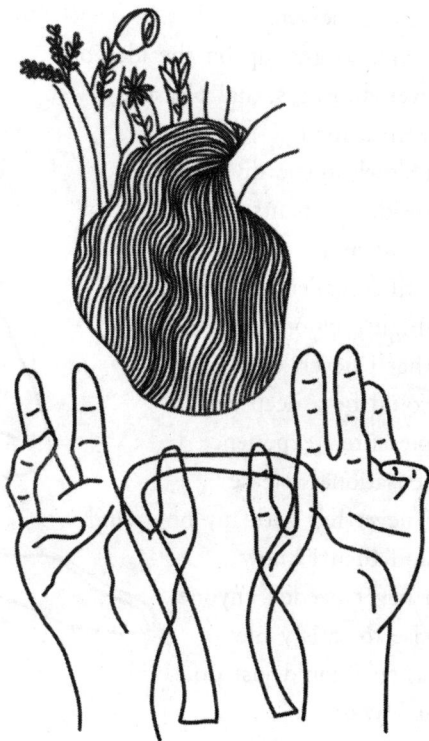

i am nineteen
about to give up on the idea of
ever finding sexual pleasure
with a man
i slowly move my hands
inside my pants
accidentally touching a tiny
ball so-called the heavenly
mighty clitoris
that i never knew
could be a deep well of
pleasure i experience a
sensational release
i never felt with my boyfriend
and then i know
i never needed anyone
else to satisfy me
when i could just do
it myself

i am liberated

in my lifetime
i have seen
many men
who have tried to
conquer their fear
and insecurity
through aggression

my advice to you
stay away from men
who have
unhealthy patterns
of expressing negative feelings
of inadequacy
towards themselves

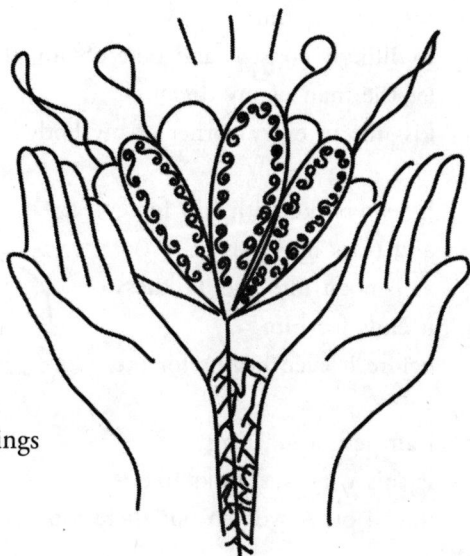

i am seventeen
for the first time
i willingly consent and take off my clothes
let the man of my dreams
kiss me in every corner of my body

he enters me with full force
and tears me apart
as i moan into the darkness
it ends for him
before it even begins for me

i am left wondering
is this what sex looks like
for all other women out there too

prioritize your pleasure first

fear is paralysing
the only way to get over fear
is to face it
to look it in the eye
and then say goodbye
i'm not afraid anymore

i'm alive
i'm alive
i'm alive

love is not just a feeling
it's an energy
created by two people
who actively choose each other
even when the sky comes
   crumbling down
and the city is on fire

soulmates
don't
exist
they
are
created
by the conscious effort
of two people who love each other
deeply
mindfully
meaningfu

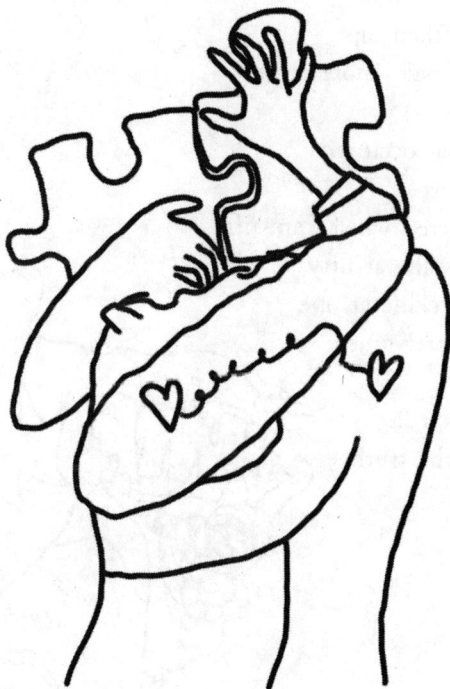

i am fifty and a half
i stare at my desk
the complete manuscript of my poems
staring back at me

i look at each poem
written in scribbles
but in chronological order
from age one to now
and i shuffle them up
so that they make more sense

the events that occurred
when i was five
make more sense when i am fifty
and somehow life at fifty
seems closer to life at one
than life at forty-nine

chronology is a lie
hindsight is the truth

158